Aya & Bobby
DISCOVER
THAILAND
Land of Smiles

Written by: Christina Kristoffersson Ameln
Illustrated by: Seonaid MacKay

To learn more about Aya & Bobby visit:

www.AyaandBobby.com

Published by Ameln & Co AB / Aya & Bobby

Copyright © Christina Ameln 2016

Printed by CreateSpace, An Amazon.com Company

Available from Amazon.com, CreateSpace.com,
and other retail outlets

Design by iraform.eu | Cover layout 2017 Melissa Dawn Baker-Nguyen

ISBN 978 91 983700 0 3

To Robert, Karl-Robert and Alexandra

For giving me love, courage and inspiration every day

Meet Aya and Bobby!

Aya is the little sister and Bobby is the big brother. Aya and Bobby love discovering and travelling to new places. They learn so much when they're away.

Join them on this exciting journey to Thailand!

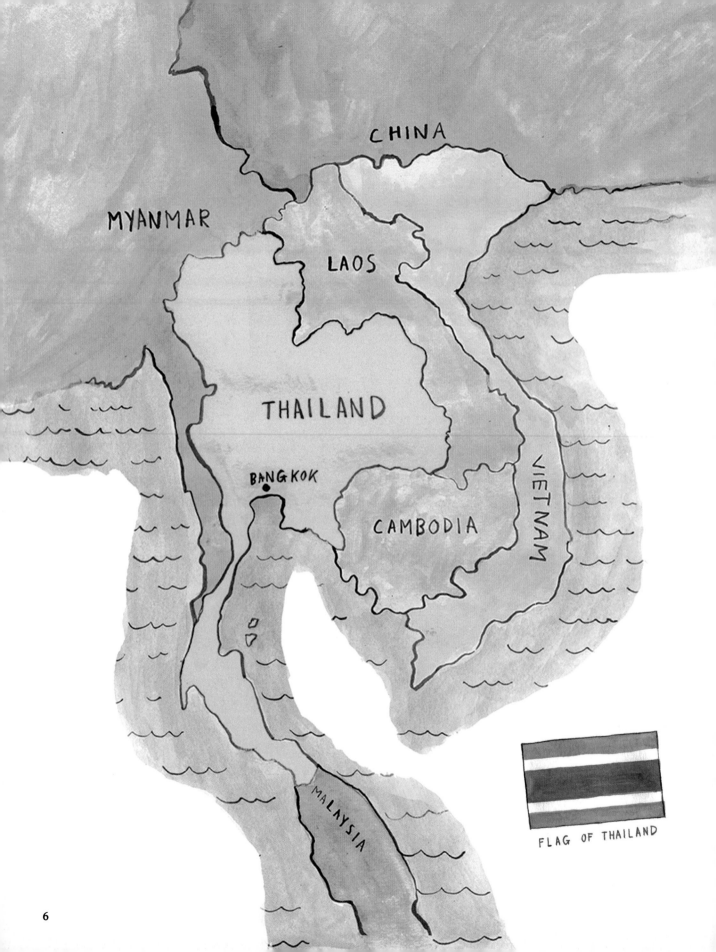

CHINA

MYANMAR

LAOS

THAILAND

BANGKOK

CAMBODIA

VIETNAM

MALAYSIA

FLAG OF THAILAND

Where is Thailand?

Thailand is located on the continent called Asia. More specifically, it's found in South-East Asia and is called the *Land of Smiles* as people from Thailand are known to smile a lot.

Thailand is also known for its beautiful beaches; delicious food; gorgeous temples; diverse animals from elephants to colourful fishes; and their love for their Royal Family.

What an amazing place to visit!

Aya and Bobby have packed their bags and included their swimwear. They've been told that they can swim every day if they want.

"I'm a bit nervous about getting water in my eyes," Bobby tells Aya.

"Bobby, make sure to bring your swimming goggles and maybe that will help. And with them on, we can also see the fish under water!"

They both decide it's a good idea to **pack their goggles!**

This time, they're travelling by airplane! It's going to be a long flight.

They decide that they'll bring their pyjamas so they can sleep on the airplane.

Aya wants to wear her pink skeleton pyjamas and Bobby his black skeleton pyjamas. They both think aloud,

"We're soo cool!"

On the plane, Aya and Bobby sit next to each other. The great thing about a long flight is that you can watch movies in your seat.

Aya likes movies with lots of singing and dancing. She often sings along and wiggles her bum bum.

Bobby likes movies that are funny. He enjoys laughing out loudly,

"HA, HA, HAAA!"

They watch and watch their movies until their
eyelids are heavy.

They really don't want to sleep as there are so many great
movies on the plane.

But finally, with the moon watching over them, Aya and
Bobby are fast asleep in their skeleton pyjamas on their
way to Thailand!

When Aya and Bobby wake up, they've arrived in Bangkok, the capital city! In the taxi from the airport to their hotel, they notice Bangkok is very busy! There are vehicles everywhere.

They also see a funny looking motorcycle with a carriage behind it. It has one wheel in front and two wheels behind. They've no idea what it is!

Aya and Bobby find out that it's called a Tuk Tuk. They laugh as they think the word is very funny and keep repeating to each other,

"Tuk, Tuk, Tuk, Tuk, Tuk Tuk!"

After a little rest at their hotel, Aya and Bobby decide that they want to explore Bangkok on the funny looking Tuk Tuk.

Aya and Bobby head out onto the street and wave to a very colourful one. They climb up at the back of the vehicle onto the passenger seat and the driver seated at the front starts the engine.

Off they go!

The engine makes a lot of noise, and they feel they're going very fast. The wind is on their faces and their hair is blowing up a storm.

They don't want to fall off the Tuk Tuk so they shout to each other,

"Hold on tight!!!!"

Their first stop is the temple!

In Thailand, the main religion is Buddhism and they pray to the image of Buddha at their temples.

Buddha was a wise man that lived a long time ago. He taught people to take care of each other and encouraged kindness.

When Aya and Bobby walk into the temple, they approach the statue of Buddha and put their hands together and respectfully say,

"Hello Buddha."

Aya and Bobby like Buddha as he teaches people to be nice to each other.

As Bobby looks around the temple, he notices people dressed in orange and realizes that they're monks. Bobby turns to Aya to say,

"Aya! Look at the monks."

Aya is not paying attention and does not hear Bobby properly. She thinks Bobby has said something else and responds,

"What! Where are the monkeys?"

They both laugh at this mistake and the monks give them a big smile having overheard the conversation.

They learn that the monks take care of the temple, pray, and study the teachings of Buddha.

Following the temple visit, Aya and Bobby decide to continue to see Bangkok on the long-tail boats. With these boats, you can go exploring on the Chao Phraya River and also weave through different canals.

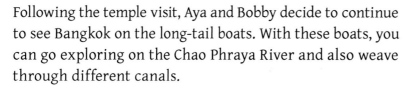

As Aya and Bobby approach the pier, they wonder why it's called a long-tail boat and realize when it approaches them.

"Bobby, it looks like a long colourful banana boat made out of wood."

"Aya, the engine at the very back of the boat makes it look like it has a tail!"

They both agree that this is indeed a funny looking boat.

Off they go at high speed. The water splashes on their faces and they laugh with a combination of fear and excitement.

ROYAL GRAND PALACE

Aya and Bobby see the beautiful Royal Grand Palace, where the Royal Family of Thailand live. They think the palace is beautiful with its decorations in gold.

TEMPLE OF DAWN

ELEPHANT

They see the Temple of Dawn and think it's one of the biggest temples they've seen.

They notice an elephant with its caretaker by the side of the water and are amazed at how big it is.

THAI HOUSES

And they see how people live by the canals – some houses are very modern and others are built in traditional Thai style.

They find Bangkok a fascinating city!

After their stay in the city, **Aya and Bobby are at the beach.** The sand is white and the sea is turquoise. It's simply one of the most beautiful beaches they've ever been on.

The first thing that Aya and Bobby do is to run into the water and make the biggest splash.

They make sure that their swimming goggles are covering their eyes. As they peer into the water, they see small fish swimming around their feet.

"Look Bobby, they're nice fish that are curious about our feet."

After spending the morning on the beach, Aya and Bobby are really hungry.

They head to the restaurant for lunch. It's perched on rocks by the beach and has a beautiful view of the sea.

Aya and Bobby are not quite sure what they'll eat. While they love travelling to new places, they're fussy eaters.

On the other hand, they know it's always important to at least taste new foods.

They decide they'll try the Pad Thai with shrimp. When it arrives in front of them, they decide they'll like this dish.

The noodles look like spaghetti and the shrimp has a lovely flavour to it.

As a joke, Aya and Bobby decide to rename the dish,

"Thai spaghetti with shrimp."

While they're eating their lunch, everyone in the restaurant suddenly stands up and points out to the sea.

"Look out there!"

"There is a dark shape swimming out to sea."

"Could it be a shark?"

Aya and Bobby hope not. They do not want to meet a shark when they're out swimming. They prefer the nice small fish that they saw earlier that day.

The restaurant owner tells them that there are different types of sharks in Thai waters.

"The Nurse and Leopard sharks are mainly plankton eaters. The Tiger shark is a meat-eating shark. However, most sharks tend not to trouble swimmers."

Aya and Bobby are relieved. That shark will not bother them and they can continue swimming in the sea.

Aya and Bobby's tummies are filled with yummy Thai food. But they insist that there is still enough space for the most important meal of the day.

"ICE CREAM!"

Aya wants chocolate ice cream. Bobby wants vanilla as he doesn't like chocolate. Aya shakes her head as she doesn't understand how Bobby cannot like chocolate.

She loves all flavours.

They notice as they walk back to the beach, that with the heat, their ice creams are melting fast.

"Hurry up!"

However, they still manage to get ice cream splotched all over their faces. They don't mind at all.

Aya and Bobby wish they can have ice cream all the time, even for breakfast!

When they're done with their ice creams, they
see a little Thai boy flying a kite.

Oh, how they wish they could do that too!

Both Aya and Bobby stand and stare, wishing from the
bottom of their hearts to fly this multi-coloured kite.
The little Thai boy notices them, smiles and says in Thai,

"Come over and play.
I will show you how to fly the kite."

They don't speak the same language but with a few
hand movements, they seem to understand each other.

Aya and Bobby take turns to borrow and fly the kite. It isn't as easy as it looks, but they soon get the hang of it.

Not only have Aya and Bobby gotten a new friend, they've also learnt

a new skill – flying a kite!

Aya and Bobby really do feel that they've had the best visit to the *Land of Smiles*.

They've explored both a big city and beach life. They feel they've learnt so much about this wonderful country.

With big smiles, Aya and Bobby wave goodbye.

"Bye bye, Thailand!
Thank you for such an amazing visit!"

Made in the USA
Las Vegas, NV
27 June 2023

73987852R00019